The  Touching Stories of Mother's Love

"Tales that Touch the Soul: Heart-Warming Stories of Love, Resilience, and Inspiration"

OP SHARMA

NOTION PRESS

NOTION PRESS

India. Singapore. Malaysia.

DEDICATION

"Dedicated to the timeless bond that transcends all realms of love, this collection of heart-touching stories is devoted to the eternal spirit of a mother's love. To the nurturer, the comforter, the unwavering source of strength and compassion—mothers who paint our lives with the hues of warmth and understanding. May these stories resonate with the profound beauty of a mother's heart, capturing the essence of an affection that knows no bounds. In honor of all the mothers who have woven the fabric of our lives with threads of love, sacrifice, and unwavering devotion. You are the true architects of our hearts."

Contents

Foreword

In every corner of the world, the bond between a mother and her child is a profound and timeless connection that transcends cultures, generations, and even language. It is a bond woven with threads of love, sacrifice, and resilience—one that shapes not only the lives of children but also the very fabric of our society. "The Heart-Touching Stories of Mother's Love" is a celebration of this extraordinary relationship, inviting readers to journey through a collection of poignant narratives that capture the essence of maternal love.

As we turn the pages of this book, we are reminded that a mother's love is not merely a feeling but an unwavering force that inspires, nurtures, and guides us through life's myriad challenges. Each story within these pages serves as a testament to the countless ways mothers express their love—through small acts of kindness, sacrifices made in silence, and the lessons imparted with gentle strength.

This collection is a tribute not only to mothers but also to the universal experiences that bind us together as human beings. Each tale resonates with the shared emotions of joy, sorrow, triumph, and hope, reflecting the intricate tapestry of motherhood. Through laughter and tears, we find solace in knowing that we are not alone in our experiences. The stories presented here remind us that the heart of a mother is a wellspring of unconditional love that endures through the trials of life.

I encourage you, dear reader, to immerse yourself in these heart-warming tales. Let them inspire you, evoke cherished memories, and deepen your appreciation for the mothers in your life. May you find comfort in the stories that echo the laughter and tears of countless mothers who have shaped the world through their love.

In a world that often rushes by, take a moment to pause, reflect, and celebrate the profound impact of a mother's love. It is a love that knows no bounds and continues to inspire us all.

With heartfelt appreciation,

Anju Sharma
Co-Founder of TurningPoint

Preface

From the moment we take our first breath, we are enveloped in the warmth of a mother's love. It is a love that nurtures, protects, and empowers us, laying the foundation for our growth and development. This book, "The Heart-Touching Stories of Mother's Love," seeks to capture the essence of this incredible bond through a collection of moving narratives that celebrate the profound impact of mothers in our lives.

In compiling these stories, I aimed to create a space for reflection on the myriad ways… mothers express their love, from the everyday sacrifices to the extraordinary acts of courage. Each story in this collection is a testament to the strength and resilience of mothers who have faced challenges with grace and tenacity, often putting their children's needs before their own. Through these heartfelt accounts, we come to understand that a mother's love is not only an emotion but a powerful force that shapes our identities and influences our journeys.

As you read these stories, I hope you find yourself transported to moments of joy, tenderness, and even heartache. Each narrative carries with it a unique perspective on the multifaceted nature of motherhood, inviting you to reflect on your own experiences and the mothers in your life—whether they are biological, adoptive, or chosen. The stories celebrate the universal themes of love, sacrifice, and connection, reminding us that while every mother's journey is different, the love they give is universal.

This collection is also an invitation to honour the mothers who have come before us and those who continue to inspire us every day. It is a tribute to the women who have faced adversity and triumph with unwavering strength, who have taught us valuable lessons, and who have instilled in us the courage to chase our dreams.

I am deeply grateful to all the contributors who shared their stories and to the readers who will embark on this journey with us. May "The Heart-Touching Stories of Mother's Love" inspire you to cherish and celebrate the mothers in your life and to recognize the profound impact they have on our hearts and souls.

With love and gratitude,

OP Sharma

Acknowledgments

"I express my deepest gratitude to the countless souls who shared their poignant narratives, allowing this collection of 'The Heart Touching Stories of Mother's Love' to come to life. To the mothers whose unwavering love inspired these tales, thank you for being the beating heart behind every word. A special acknowledgment to those who selflessly contributed their experiences, adding layers of emotion and authenticity to these stories. I extend my appreciation to my family…. A wonderful mother, a wonderful wife, and a blessed daughter "ARPITA" and friends for their endless support and encouragement throughout this heartfelt journey. Lastly, to the readers, may these stories resonate with the universal beauty of a Mother's Love and serve as a tribute to the extraordinary bonds we share with the maternal figures in our lives."

Prologue

In every culture, in every corner of the globe, one truth remains universal: the love of a mother is unmatched and irreplaceable. It is a bond forged in the quiet moments of tenderness, the loud bursts of laughter, and the unyielding support offered during life's toughest challenges. This love, often expressed in a thousand small gestures, shapes our lives in ways that words alone cannot capture.

"The Heart-Touching Stories of Mother's Love" is an exploration of this incredible bond—a collection of narratives that reveal the depth, complexity, and beauty of motherhood. Within these pages, you will find stories that resonate with the familiar warmth of a mother's embrace, the gentle guidance of a loving hand, and the sacrifices made in the name of love. Each tale is a reminder that mothers are the unsung heroes of our lives, whose influence often goes unrecognized but is deeply felt.

As we navigate the ups and downs of life, it is often our mothers who provide the compass, helping us find our way home. They teach us resilience, compassion, and the importance of nurturing our dreams. They are our first teachers, our biggest supporters, and our greatest sources of strength. The stories shared in this book reflect these truths, showcasing the diverse experiences of mothers from all walks of life—each with their own unique story of love and devotion.

In a world that often moves too quickly, it is essential to pause and reflect on the impact that mothers have on our lives and the legacies they leave behind. This collection invites you to do just that. As you read these stories, I encourage you to connect with the emotions they evoke, to remember your own experiences with maternal love, and to honour the mothers who have shaped your journey.

May these heart-touching stories serve as a celebration of the remarkable women who have given us so much, and may they inspire you to cherish and appreciate the love that has been woven into the fabric of your life.

Welcome to a journey of love, sacrifice, and unforgettable moments—a journey that begins with the heart of a mother.

With love,

OP Sharma

Chapter - 1

"The Boy and His Mother"

"A mother's love is the fuel that enables a normal human being to do the impossible"

Ron was a 12-year-old boy who lived with his mother and father. He was happy with his life going to school and playing with friends. He threw tantrums like any other kid of his age. His mother was a homemaker. She did not complain about her tantrums and considered them normal.

Ron was happy as his school had declared holidays for five consecutive days. It was a streak of national holidays, the government announced. His father and mother were also happy. After a long period, they had time to relax and go on a vacation.

His mother and father took Ron to a nearby beach, had a great dinner in a big hotel, and watched a movie. Two days passed with so much enjoyment and peace.

The Boy's Bill for Service to Mother...

Three days were left. Ron's mother decided to clean the house. It was a good time when his father could also lend a hand. She would then be able to clean the house properly with everyone's help.

She asked Ron, "Will you help with the cleaning?" Ron agreed and did his best. He dusted the furniture, cut the grass on the lawn, watered the plants, went shopping to buy groceries with a list his mother prepared, and helped his mother, to dry clothes.

Ron Doing Chores.........

His mother was stunned to see Ron helping her so much. All the duties assigned were executed with utmost care. She was impressed that Ron was learning to be a part of the family. She was happy that he was growing up to become a mature person.

Ron was scribbling on a piece of paper. Her mother fondled his hair. He handed a note to her mother. She could not look at the note as she was busy making food.

When she was done, she saw the note and was surprised. It mentioned service charges for all the work he had done. His mother thought, when did her son become so professional? It was a little depressing, and she had to teach her son a lesson.

The Mother Taught a Lesson.......

Her mother attached another note to her son's note. It mentioned:

- Carrying you in my belly for nine months – no charge

- Taking care when you are sick – no charge

- Soothing you when you are scared or annoyed – no charge

- Praying for your health and happiness every day – no charge

- Taking care of all your needs – no charge

She handed the note to her son. Ron realized what a mistake he had made. He apologized to his mother immediately and hugged her tightly.

Moral of the Story:

"The Story of a Mother's Unconditional Love is... you cannot

put a price on a mother's love. It is unconditional, no matter what. She will always love her child and shower him with care. The son realized his responsibilities toward her mother. This moral makes the readers think of the unconditional love of a mother and realize their duties too."

Chapter - 2

"Love of A Mother"

"A mother's sacrifice is a reflection of her unwavering faith in her children's potential."

Once there was a child who lived with her mother.

The kid used to hate her mother because she only had a single eye.

She used to cook so that she could earn some money and pay her son's school fees.

One day the mother went to his kid's school for a parent-teacher meeting.

The kid feels so embarrassed that he ran out of the class.

One of the kids said, "Eeu, your mother has only one eye."

The kid ran home, and when his mother reached home, he started shouting and saying, "Why you are like this, people make fun of me, so why won't you die?"

After listening to this, she didn't say anything.

The child studied hard, and he got a job abroad.

There he got married and had kids with all the comforts of life.

One day his mother came to meet him.

This was the first time when she was going to meet his son and her grandchildren.

As she rang the bell and stood by the door, her grandchildren opened the door and started **laughing**.

They didn't know who she was.

The man came and started screaming at her mother, "How can you come to my house and how dare you scare my children, go away."

She replied, "Oh, I am sorry I knocked on the wrong door."

One day the boy got a letter from his college about a reunion.

He was very excited and attended the reunion.

After that, he went to the old shack where he used to live with his mother.

One of the neighbors told him that she died and gave him a letter for his son.

He opened the letter, "My dearest son, I think of you all the time, and I am sorry that I came to your house and scared your children. And I am really sorry for constantly embarrassing you, but I want you to know one thing. When you were a kid, you met with an accident and lost an eye. As your mother, I couldn't see you growing up with a single eye, so I gave you mine. Take care, my dear love."

Moral of the Story:

"A mother's love can never end, and it will be there from the beginning till the end. We see in life how children, when they grew up, didn't respect their parents and often they used to tell the parents to leave the house and to get lost from their lives.

The mother is like a garden, and the father is like a mountain.

If you understand the importance of a parent's love, then you will forget *the importance of goods and wealth. 'She gives all she has to us, and more'."*

the importance of goods and wealth. 'She gives all she has to us, and more'."

Chapter - 3

"Mother's Embrace"

"A mother's love is the Greatest Gift a child can receive. It is the one constant in an ever-changing world."

In a small town nestled between rolling hills and meandering streams, lived a woman named Clara. She wasn't adorned with riches or adorned in the latest fashions, but her heart overflowed with an abundance of love.

Clara had a son named Jacob, a spirited and curious boy with a penchant for adventure. Life, however, had dealt them a challenging hand. Jacob was born with a rare condition that required frequent medical attention and brought moments of uncertainty into their lives.

Amidst the hospital visits and sleepless nights, Clara remained an unwavering pillar of strength for her son. Her days were spent juggling between work, doctor appointments, and creating a warm and loving home for Jacob. Despite the challenges, Clara's love for her son shone brightly.

One winter evening, as the town was blanketed in a layer of snow, Jacob expressed a simple desire – to build a snowman together. Clara, with a tired but loving smile, agreed. They bundled up in layers of warm clothing, and with mittened hands, they began shaping the snow into a delightful snowman.

As they worked side by side, laughter echoed through the frosty air. For a brief moment, the weight of their worries lifted, and the pure joy of the present enveloped them. The snowman stood tall as a testament to their shared love and resilience.

In the years that followed, Jacob faced numerous challenges, but Clara's love remained a constant source of comfort. She became not just a mother but a beacon of hope, teaching Jacob the strength that lies within a mother's embrace.

Moral of the Story:

"This heart-touching story is a reminder that a mother's love transcends all obstacles. Clara's unwavering devotion to her son, even in the face of adversity, paints a *poignant picture of the extraordinary bond between a mother and her child."*

Chapter - 4

"Mother's Unconditional Love"

"A mother's love is the ultimate sacrifice, for she gives everything she has for her children."

There was a couple, who had a son named Rohit. They lived happily ever after and their child Rohit grew into a young lad. And one day the couple decided to marry their son. After Rohit got married, he started feeling irritated with his parents and when his father died one day, he decided to send his Mother to an old age home. Even after his mother did not want to go to the old age home, he by force sent her to a place where they might not have access even to the basic amenities of life.

He used to visit his Mother at the old age home once a week. One day he came to know that his mother was seriously ill and she was left only with a few hours of her life. He decided to visit his mother that day and found her lying on the bed. Out of nowhere his heart started feeling bad for himself that he had not treated his mother the way she had always treated him.

He asked his mother if he could do something in her last time that would make her happy. Upon which his mother replied that, dear son, please install some fans in the rooms here, as there isn't any fan in any of the rooms of this home. And also buy a fridge for the old people living here. Many a time people living here have to sleep without food as it gets spoiled many times for the lack of a fridge. And, son, for that reason, I had to sleep without food for many days. Son, being perplexed, asked why you are asking me for all these today when you are left only with few hours.

The Mother replied to Son, I am worried that you will not be able to live here comfortably when your son will one day send you here. So, I want everything before you come here to be mended. The son's heart was overwhelmed to hear these words from his mother. This is how a mother's love is!! It did not demand anything!!

Moral of the Story:

"A mother is someone who without thinking about her own interests, nurtures her child's interests. She is the one who will do everything to keep alive her children's dreams. No matter what she will stand behind and protect her child in all the circumstances."

Chapter - 5

"Mother's Blessing"

"The relationship between a mother and child is one of the strongest and Most loving bonds in the world."

There once was a little boy who lived with his mother. They were very poor. The boy was very handsome and extremely smart. As he grew older, he became even more handsome and smarter. However, his mother always remained sad.

Once, the boy asked his mother, "Mother, why are you always sad?" Mother replied, "Son, a fortune teller once told me that whoever has teeth like yours will become very famous." Then the boy asked, "Will you not like it if I become famous?"

"Oh, my son! What kind of mother wouldn't like it if her son became famous? I'm always sad because I keep thinking that you will forget me and leave me once you become famous."

Upon hearing this, the boy started to cry. He stood there in front of his mother for a while and then ran out of the house. He picked up a rock from outside and smashed his front two teeth. He started to bleed from his mouth.

His mother ran out and was shocked to see what he had done. She asked, "Son! What did you do?" In reply, the boy held his mother's hands and said, "Mother, if these teeth cause you pain and make you sad, I don't want them. They are of no use to me. I don't want to be famous with these teeth. I want to be famous by serving you and through your blessings…

Moral of the Story:

"True love and devotion often involves self-sacrifice. The boy demonstrates that genuine success and fulfilment come from prioritizing the happiness and well-being of loved ones over personal ambitions. In this case, the boy values his mother's happiness more than the fame that could come with his physical appearance, showing that love and selflessness are more important than superficial achievement

Chapter - 6

"The Unseen Gift"

"A mother is she who can take the place of all others but whose place no one else can take."

In a quiet village nestled between emerald hills, lived a woman named Maria. She was known throughout the community for her kindness, compassion, and, above all, her unwavering love for her daughter, Isabella.

Isabella, a spirited and curious young girl, had always admired her mother's ability to find joy in simple things. Every day, after completing her chores, Maria would gather the children of the village for storytelling. Her tales were filled with lessons of kindness, empathy, and the magic that exists in the bonds we share.

One day, Isabella approached her mother with a curious question, "Mother, why do you always emphasize the importance of love and understanding in your stories?"

Maria smiled, her eyes filled with the wisdom that only a mother could possess. She replied, "My dear Isabella, love is the most powerful force in the world. It can heal wounds, bridge gaps, and make the ordinary extraordinary. In every tale I share, there is a hidden gift – a reminder that the love we give and receive shapes the world around us."

One summer day, tragedy struck the village. A severe storm damaged crops, leaving many families in distress. The villagers worked tirelessly to rebuild their homes and replant their fields. Isabella, inspired by her mother's stories, decided to help in any way she could.

With Maria's guidance, Isabella organized a community gathering to share resources and support one another. The village began to heal, not just physically but emotionally, as the bonds of love and unity grew stronger.

As Isabella witnessed the positive impact of their collective efforts, she understood the moral her mother had embedded in every story: the true magic lies in the love we extend to others during times of need.

Years passed, and Isabella carried her mother's lessons into adulthood. She became a source of strength and comfort for the villagers, just like Maria. The legacy of love and compassion lived on, illustrating that a mother's love, when nurtured and shared, has the power to create a world where kindness becomes the unseen gift that connects us all.

Moral of the Story:

"The moral of the story is that love, kindness, and empathy have the power to transform challenges into opportunities for growth and unity."

Chapter - 7

"The Warmth of a Mother's Love"
"No matter your age, you will always need your mom."

It had been more than an hour since the train had screeched to a halt at the small station. Running out of patience, Aditya got up from his seat to find out the cause of the delay. As he approached the doorway, he noticed it was raining outside.

He went back to his seat and lay down with his bag under his head. Before long, he had drifted off. Suddenly, he was jolted out of sleep by a woman tugging at his sleeve. He sat up and saw a middle-aged woman with dishevelled appearance and dirty clothes, clutching his handbag in her hand. The train had pulled out of the station and was speeding by then. Aditya, in his sleep, didn't realize when his handbag had slipped from under his head and fallen to the floor.

He hurriedly took the bag from her to check if his wallet and belongings were in place. As soon as he opened the bag, he was surprised to see his mother's shawl inside. Everything else in the bag was in order. He took out the shawl and his thoughts drifted to the night before, when he was packing his bags before going to bed. His mother had brought her shawl and had insisted on putting it in his bag. She had said, "If it rains, it may get cold."

He remembered feeling a bit annoyed and had taken the shawl out of the bag. But it was still with him. "Maa must have kept it back after I had slept off," he thought to himself.

After a while, when Aditya got up to get some water, he realized his body was burning with fever. Feeling helpless, he called up his mother, "Mom, last night you wanted to give me a pack of medicines…"

Before he could finish, his mother cut in, "Do you have a headache?"

Aditya didn't want her to worry about his fever, so he said yes.

His mother said, "Take a pill for your headache. I have put it in the front pocket of your handbag. I have also put in medicine for fever, just in case. And eat something. I have packed a sandwich and kept it in your bag."

He was in awe of his mother's care and concern. He ate the sandwich, took the medicine, and fell asleep in the warmth of his mother's shawl.

Aditya woke up a few hours later feeling better than before. As he got up to stretch his legs, he noticed a woman sitting near the gangway, cradling a child in her arms. Their worn-out clothes did little to shield them against the cold gusts of wind sweeping in from the open windows. He realized she was the same woman who had woken him earlier to give him back his bag.

Without thinking twice, Aditya took his mother's shawl and wrapped it around the shivering baby.

He noticed how comfortably the child now slept, wrapped in the love and affection of not one, but two mothers.

Moral of the Story:

"Love, care, and kindness transcend personal boundaries and can create a ripple effect. Aditya's mother's care for him extends beyond

his immediate needs, and he, in turn, passes on that care and warmth to a stranger in need. The story highlights the importance of empathy and selflessness, showing that small acts of kindness can make a significant difference in the lives of others. It also reflects how a mother's love is universal, nurturing not only her own child but also inspiring her child to care for others."

Chapter - 8

"Giver Not Acquirer"

**"A mother's sacrifice is the purest form of selflessness,
for she gives without expecting anything in return."**

After having a lot of success in his career a young man felt an urge to repay back his mother for all that she had done for him. So, he asked her "Mom what can I give you? What can I do for you? I sincerely want to repay you for all the sacrifices you have made for me and all the love you have showered upon me".

Mother looked surprised and said "Why do you think about it? It was my duty so I did it. You don't have to repay me. Even if you want to, there is no way a man can ever repay his mother.

Despite her continuous refusal to ask for anything, he continued to persist. To put an end to the discussion, she said" All right, if you must, then tonight you sleep on my bed with me as you used to when you were a baby".

He said, "That's a strange thing to ask for but if it pleases you, I will".

As soon as he fell asleep, the mother got up brought a bucket of water, and poured a mug full of water on his side. Feeling disturbed by the wetness under him, in his sleep he moves away to the other side of the bed. As he settled down, his mother poured another mug of water on the other side. In his slumber, he tried to find space towards the footpost of the bed.

Sometimes later he woke up feeling that this part of the bed too was damp. He got up and saw his mother with the mug in her hand.

He asked, "What are you doing Mom? Why don't you let me sleep? How do you expect me to sleep in a wet bed?

Mother said, "I slept with you when you wetted the bed in the night. I changed your clothes and moved you to the dry part of the bed, while I slept on the wet side. You wanted to repay me…. can you sleep here even for one night with me on a damp bed? If you can, I'll take it that you have repaid me.

Moral of the Story:

"Of all the debts of the world, the one that can never be repaid is the one you owe to your mother. You can never repay the love, care, and time your mother gave to bring you up. You are a part of her flesh and blood, don't forget this because she never forgets it.

Be a giver, not an acquirer, especially with your parents.

Chapter - 9

"Undying Mother's Courage"

"A mother's arms are more comforting than anyone else's."

In a small village nestled between rolling hills and meandering streams, there lived a woman named Ananya. Her days were filled with simplicity, yet her heart held a story of unwavering love that resonated with everyone who knew her.

Ananya was the mother of two children, Aarav and Aanya. Aarav, the older of the two, was a bright and curious boy, while Aanya, the younger one, was a sweet and gentle soul. Ananya's days were spent tending to her children, and her nights were filled with lullabies that echoed through the village.

Life, however, had its challenges for Ananya. Her husband, a humble farmer, had passed away when the children were still very young. Despite the grief that weighed on her heart, Ananya embraced her role as a single mother with grace and determination.

One day, tragedy struck the village as a harsh storm swept through, leaving a trail of destruction. Aarav, in his attempt to save the family's livestock, got caught in the fury of the storm. Ananya, with the strength that only a mother possesses, rushed to his rescue.

The villagers, witnessing the unfolding drama, could do nothing but watch as Ananya battled the fierce winds and torrential rain to reach her son. With every step, she called out his name, her voice cutting through the howling storm.

Miraculously, Ananya reached Aarav and shielded him with her own body. The storm seemed to relent as if nature itself recognized the power of a mother's love. The villagers, moved by the selflessness and courage displayed by Ananya, joined in the effort to bring them both to safety.

In the aftermath of the storm, as the village began to rebuild, Aarav and Aanya clung to their mother with a newfound appreciation. The ordeal had not only brought them physically closer but had also revealed the depth of love that Ananya held for them.

The story of Ananya and her children spread beyond the village, becoming a testament to the resilience and boundless love of a mother. Ananya's heart, though scarred by loss, continued to beat with a rhythm of love that inspired those who knew her.

Moral of the Story:

"The tale of Ananya serves as a reminder that a mother's love can weather the fiercest storms, conquer the greatest challenges, and illuminate even the darkest paths. It is a love that transcends time and circumstance, leaving an indelible mark on the hearts of those fortunate enough to be embraced by its warmth."

Chapter - 10

"Bridge of Mother's love"

"A mother's love is the glue that holds a family together. It is the source of strength and resilience that carries us through tough times."

In the bustling city of Harmonyville, there lived a single mother named Radha. She worked tirelessly as a nurse, devoting her days to caring for others in the hospital. Her evenings, however, were dedicated to her daughter, Mira, a bright-eyed girl with dreams as vast as the starlit sky.

Radha's love for Mira knew no bounds. Despite the challenges life threw their way, she made sure Mira always felt secure and loved. One day, Radha received news that she had been chosen for a prestigious nursing program abroad — an opportunity that would open new doors for both her and Mira.

Excitement filled the air as Radha shared the news with Mira. However, amidst the joy, a shadow of concern crossed Mira's face. The prospect of her mother being away for an extended period weighed heavily on her young heart. Sensing her daughter's anxiety, Radha sat Mira down and spoke from the depth of her soul.

"Sweetheart," Radha began, "my love for you is boundless, and distance can never diminish that. This journey is not just for me; it's for us, for our future. I will carry your love with me every step of the way, and my heart will always beat in harmony with yours."

The day came for Radha to embark on her journey, leaving Mira in the care of her grandmother. As the plane took off, Radha looked out of the window, sending silent messages of love to Mira. Meanwhile, Mira found solace in the letters and video messages her mother sent regularly, each filled with warmth and encouragement.

Months passed, and Radha's absence became a testament to the enduring strength of a mother's love. Mira, though missing her deeply, understood the sacrifices her mother was making for their shared dreams.

One day, Radha returned home, having successfully completed her program. The reunion between mother and daughter was filled with tears, laughter, and an overwhelming sense of accomplishment. The challenges they faced had only strengthened the bond between them.

Radha's journey taught Mira the importance of perseverance, sacrifice, and the enduring strength that love provides. Their story became an inspiration for many in Harmonyville, emphasizing the profound lessons that can be learned through the unwavering love between a mother and her child.

Moral of the Story:

"The moral of this story is that a mother's love transcends physical presence. Radha's sacrifice for Mira's future exemplifies the selflessness and resilience inherent in a mother's heart. Love, when nurtured and sustained, has the power to bridge any distance and withstand the tests of time."

Chapter - 11

"Eternal Threads of Love"

"A mother's love is like no other. It's a bond that cannot be broken, a love that cannot be explained, and a feeling that will last a lifetime."

In the heart of a serene village, there lived a mother named Sita, whose love for her son, Raj, was as timeless as the rising sun. Sita was known not just for her nurturing spirit but also for the quiet strength she carried, a strength that became the foundation of their simple yet harmonious life.

As Raj grew older, his curiosity led him beyond the village borders, seeking adventures in distant lands. Sita, though filled with maternal worry, allowed him the freedom to explore the world. One day, however, news reached the village of a perilous journey Raj had undertaken, and Sita's heart quivered with fear.

Driven by an unshakable mother's instinct, Sita embarked on a journey to find her son, traversing mountains, crossing rivers, and facing challenges that tested her resolve. Her love was a guiding light, leading her through the darkest nights and the most treacherous paths.

After months of relentless pursuit, Sita finally found Raj in a remote village, weary and disheartened. With tearful eyes, she embraced him, and in that moment, the world seemed to stand still. Sita's love had transcended distance, time, and hardship to reunite a lost son with his mother.

Moral of the Story:

"Eternal Threads of Love" teaches us that a mother's love is an unwavering force capable of overcoming any obstacle. Sita's determination and sacrifice highlight the profound depth of a mother's commitment to her child. It emphasizes the enduring nature of love, connecting hearts across distances and challenges. Just as Sita's love guided her through the toughest *trials, the story encourages us to appreciate and reciprocate the selfless love mothers shower upon their children, recognizing it as a powerful force that binds families together."*

Chapter - 12

"The Sacred Lullaby"

"Life doesn't come with a manual; it comes with a mother"

In the heart of a quaint town nestled between rolling hills and fragrant meadows, there lived a woman named Leela. She was a mother with a heart as vast as the open sky, and her love for her daughter, Aisha, was a melody that echoed through their small home.

Leela was a weaver, known for creating intricate patterns with threads of vibrant colours. Her days were spent crafting beautiful textiles, but her evenings were dedicated to Aisha, whom she cherished as the most precious creation of her life.

Aisha, a spirited young girl with dreams that danced like butterflies, found solace in the comforting lullabies Leela sang every night. These songs were not just melodies; they were a magical tapestry woven with love and care, creating a cocoon of warmth around the mother-daughter duo.

One day, a sudden illness befell Leela, casting a shadow over their once-vibrant home. As Leela's strength waned, Aisha became the pillar of support, doing her best to emulate the love and care her mother had showered upon her. The roles reversed, and it was now Aisha's turn to weave threads of comfort around her ailing mother.

As the days passed, Leela's condition deteriorated, and the once lively home echoed with the sombre notes of reality. In her final moments, Leela gathered every ounce of strength to hold Aisha close and whispered, "My love for you, my dear, is like an eternal lullaby. Even when I'm gone, the melody will linger in your heart, guiding you through life's journey."

Aisha, though heartbroken, clung to her mother's words. In the quiet moments that followed, she found solace in the memories of the sacred lullabies and the love that had been woven into the fabric of their lives.

Moral of the Story:

"The Sacred Lullaby" teaches us that a mother's love is a timeless melody that continues to resonate even when she is physically absent. Leela's lullabies symbolize the enduring nature of a mother's influence, nurturing and guiding her child through life's joys and sorrows. The story encourages us to appreciate the profound impact of a mother's love, recognizing it as a source of strength and comfort that transcends the boundaries of time and space."

Chapter - 13

"The Blossoming Garden of Love"

**"A mother is … she who can take the place
of all others but whose place no one else can take."**

In a quaint village surrounded by lush green fields, there lived a mother named Ananya. Her love for her daughter, Kiara, was like a garden that flourished with every passing day. Ananya, a woman of kindness and grace, devoted her life to nurturing not just plants in her garden but also the tender heart of her beloved child.

Ananya's small cottage was adorned with flowers of all hues, each blossom holding a story of love. Kiara, a curious and imaginative girl, often found solace in the vibrant garden her mother had cultivated. It was a sanctuary where the whispers of the wind blended with the laughter of blossoms.

One day, as the village faced a severe drought, Ananya's garden wilted, and the once lively colours turned pale. The villagers, burdened by the scarcity of water, were forced to prioritize survival over the aesthetics of nature. Ananya, however, made a choice that left the villagers in awe.

She sacrificed the limited water she had to revive her garden, believing that the beauty and life it brought to her daughter's world were worth more than the immediate needs of the village. Kiara, witnessing her mother's selfless act, learned a profound lesson about the priorities of love and sacrifice.

As the garden slowly revived, so did the spirits of the villagers. Ananya's gesture of love and sacrifice touched their hearts, and they began to contribute to the well-being of the entire community. The once withered fields started to bloom with renewed life.

Moral of the Story:

"The Blossoming Garden of Love" illustrates that a mother's love is not only nurturing but also has the power to inspire acts of selflessness and kindness in others. Ananya's devotion to her garden becomes a metaphor for the transformative impact of love on the world around us. The story

encourages us to appreciate the beauty that love brings into our lives and to recognize that acts of sacrifice for the well-being of those we cherish can create a ripple effect, fostering a more compassionate and harmonious community."

Chapter - 14

"A Tapestry of Love"

**"A mother's love knows no boundaries,
no limitations, and no conditions."**

In the heart of a quiet town, there lived a mother named Priya. Her love for her daughter, Naina, was a masterpiece, woven with threads of devotion and warmth. Priya, a skilled weaver, not only crafted vibrant textiles for the villagers but also wove a unique tapestry of love into the fabric of their lives.

Naina, a spirited young girl, often marvelled at the intricate patterns her mother created. Little did she know that the most beautiful tapestry was the one woven around her heart by Priya's unconditional love.

One day, as Naina faced the challenges of adolescence, she felt the tapestry of their relationship stretching thin. Misunderstandings and conflicts arose, causing ripples in the once harmonious weave. Priya, sensing her daughter's turmoil, decided to mend the tapestry with patience, understanding, and a mother's boundless love.

Through heartfelt conversations and shared laughter, Priya and Naina began to repair the delicate threads. The tapestry, though scarred, became even more beautiful, illustrating the resilience of a mother's love in the face of adversity.

As Naina grew older, she realized the depth of her mother's sacrifices and the strength of the bond they shared. The tapestry, now a testament to their enduring love, adorned the walls of their home like a living work of art.

Moral of the Story:

"A Tapestry of Love" conveys that a mother's love is a continuous and evolving masterpiece, capable of weathering the storms of life. Priya's dedication to repairing the tapestry of her relationship with Naina teaches us the importance of patience, understanding, and the transformative power of love. The story encourages us to value the *intricate threads of connection with our loved ones, recognizing that, through love and effort, even the most fragile bonds can be strengthened into something enduring and beautiful."*

Chapter - 15

"The Echo of a Mother's Love"

"A mother's love is a force of nature that cannot be tamed or contained. it is a love that is boundless and infinite."

In a small village embraced by emerald hills and golden fields, there lived a mother named Lila. Her love for her son, Arjun, was a melody that resonated through the valleys and soared with the winds. Lila, a woman of quiet strength, dedicated her days to nurturing Arjun's dreams and shaping his character with the gentle touch of a mother's love.

Arjun, a spirited young boy, found solace in the embrace of his mother's love. Whether through comforting lullabies or encouraging words, Lila was always there, a steady presence in his world. As Arjun grew, so did his ambitions, and he set out to explore the world beyond the familiar borders of their village.

One day, as Arjun embarked on a journey to pursue his dreams, he faced the tumultuous waves of life. Challenges and setbacks tested his resilience, and in moments of despair, he felt the echo of his mother's love in the memories they had woven together.

In his darkest hour, when the road seemed insurmountable, Arjun received a letter from Lila. Her words were a balm to his wounded spirit, a reminder that no matter how far he travelled, the echo of her love would guide him home.

Through trials and triumphs, Arjun persevered, fuelled by the unwavering support imprinted on his heart by Lila's love. As he achieved his dreams and stood on the summit of his accomplishments, he realized that the true measure of success was not in the destination but in the journey, enriched by the echo of a mother's love.

Moral of the Story:

"The Echo of a Mother's Love" underscores the enduring impact of a mother's love on the lives of her children. Lila's love became a guiding force, providing strength and solace to Arjun in moments of adversity. The story emphasizes that a mother's love, though intangible, leaves an indelible

mark, shaping the character and resilience of her children as they navigate the journey of life. It encourages us to cherish the echoes of love that resonate in our hearts, for they are a source of inspiration and strength in our pursuit of dreams."

Chapter - 16

"Scars in Your Life...!"

"A mother's love is like no other. It's a bond that
cannot be broken, a love that cannot be explained,
And a feeling that will last a lifetime."

On a hot summer day, a little boy and his mother were inside a lake house. Little boy decided to go for a swim in the lake behind his house. Boy was excited to go into the lake and swim in cool lake so he just ran out.

The boy went onto the lake and swam far without realizing that he swam right into the middle of that lake. The boy's mother looked out of the window and saw an alligator approaching towards his son.

As she saw both of them getting closer to each other, she ran toward little boy and yelled as loud as she could. She shouted about alligator approaching him and asked him to swim back towards house.

Hearing the voice of his mother, boy got

alarmed and u-turned to swim towards his mother but it was too late. Just as the mother reached her little boy and grabbed his arm, at the same moment alligator snatched his legs. Then began a tug-of-war between the two. Alligator was too strong but the mother was too passionate to let her son go.

At the same time, a farmer happens to pass by and hears the scream of a little boy and his mother. The farmer raced toward lake took his aim at alligator and shot him.

Remarkably, after getting treated for weeks in hospital boy survived.

A newspaper reporter came to interview boy after the incident and asked him about the incident. The boy lifted his pants from his legs which were extremely scarred by the vicious attack of the animal.

But then, with pride he said to reporters, "look at my arms. I have great scars on my arms too."

Newspaper reporter, "Why these scars are great?"

The boy replied, "I have these scars on my arm because my mom wouldn't let go..."

Moral of the Story:

"Similarly, in our life we have scars from painful past. Sometimes, we foolishly get into difficult situations and we forget that the enemy is waiting. That's when tug of war begins between life and god. That's why some wounds we have because god wouldn't let go. We should be very grateful to god and mother for being there with us."

Chapter - 17

"Unconditional Love"

"A mother's resilience is like a tree in a storm, bending but never breaking."

A mother who lost her husband was left all alone to take care of her loving child. She had to work for her and her son's living, she had no other option as she was poor she could not afford a healthy lifestyle. She was staying with her sister-in-law who was unfit to work outside.

Mom was feeding her son some food and when the kid always refused to eat.... she showed him the moon and told her kid that she would bring that moon one day to him so that he could eat all his food.

Days passed by as the child was growing, the child started gaining knowledge and whenever he used to see any men on the television, he casually showed his mother and says Mom it's Dad, I saw Dad on the TV. Mom just sighs off by saying no it's not your Dad.

Mom took very good care of her son and made him a successful businessman where he was so rich that he could sit and eat for the next two generations.

One fine day, the son walks down the staircase and all his servants gossip saying that their boss is coming. He proudly lifts his head and walks down the staircase. In the meanwhile, he had called for the best doctors to take care of his sick mother.

One of the doctors informs him that his mother is very serious and she is also not eating her food which is being served to her. The son just yells at the doctors by saying that he does not care. He asks his aunty (mom's sister-in-law) as to why that old lady (mother) is behaving so childish and torturing everyone.

His aunty slaps him and informs him, wake up, this is the same mother who took care of you when you could not walk, this is the same mother who fed you food even when you used to refuse to eat. If your mother had to say why is my stupid son not eating his food and leaving you, you would not have been the man that you are today.

She just needs you near her at this time. She just wants you to ask her if she ate her breakfast, lunch, or dinner. That's all she wants. Then see she will get up and she will be fine. All she needs is just two minutes of your time.

The son fell down on his knees crying and asking for pardon from God.

Moral of the Story:

"Mother's love is a treasure, you need to jewel it or else it will be worthless to feel for it once it is lost."

Chapter - 18

"Mother's Love Worth a Sacrifice"

"A mother's love for her child is like nothing else in the world. It knows no law, no pity, it dares all things, and crushes down remorselessly all that stands in its path."

A mother is the person who better defines this proverb. The mother, this refined creature, who does everything to make her surroundings a true world of comfort and takes care of every detail of Life.

Esther will never forget that day her mom was a week away from giving birth to his little brother Joshua. She was preparing me to go to school. She wanted to change her top, so she asked me for a hand, at the level of her belly I noticed a large bandaged injury surrounded by stretch marks. I was very scared and asked her: ......" But Mum, how did you get a huge injury like that, what happened to you wait I'm going to call Aunty Marcellin, so that she'll take care of you. She replied, "No Esther, you must go to school". I replied, "But mummy … are you out of your head with what you ask me there, go to school filled with you and you're hurt like that? She said to me with a smile on her face: Masoro (which means dad's princess) this is not a hurt it's my best * accomplishment * … accomplishment. I asked again with great curiosity as I am curious I like to discover and learn. She replied, "Yes, my body cannot allow me to give a normal delivery. So, doctors offered me whether to kill the baby and adopt a child or pass by the caesarean method that is to say you out by my belly instead of the genitals. She… continues saying … What you see here in a bandage is because your little brother Joshua has come out here and it is not yet dry, your sister and you too also were born in this way".

I was only 7 years old at that time the only words I said were, "Mom do not cry…. it will pass, I'm going to school and I'll bring back your biscuits you'll eat and this injury will disappear". Today I realize that it was a great promise I gave to my mother. to make my mother happy and proud through the education she gives me and make her forget all the pains of the past

The method of caesarean delivery in the Democratic Republic of the Congo at that time was very risky. It was a method done just by a scalpel and a needle. The woman was in danger of cancer, and the caesarean section took half of her belly.

My mother accepts all this just to give me life. Nowadays all women want to have size 36, she accepted a deformed body and stretch marks she accepted Scars on her stomach for all her life just to get me.

One day in the living room I asked her why she did not wear fancy clothes or luxury accessories, she replied that her luxurious life is the education she gives us. Her only goal is to put ourselves in a favourable climate for our future. What love can be compared to a mother's love?

She's not highly educated and does not have a good French accent, still, she remains the best teacher that can exist. And that in all areas of life. She does not know or wear Gucci, Channel, Louboutin, or Berberie...; She remains the most beautiful in the world… her intelligence is comparable to the new technology. She finds a solution to everything.

Moral of the Story:

"That's a mother! ... to all the moms of the world! ... to all creatures that give real meaning to life! ... all the sublime creatures who understand things in their fine details! ... all these sublime creatures who! understand everything from their own perspective! ... to you the woman always in honour."

Chapter - 19

"Mother and Son"
"A mother's love is more beautiful than any fresh flower."

My mother used to ask me what the most important part of the body is. Through the years I would guess what I thought was the correct Answer. When I was younger, I thought sound was very important to us as humans, so I said, 'My ears, Mommy.'

She said, 'No. Many people are deaf. But you keep thinking about it and I will ask you again soon.' Several years passed before she asked me again. Since making my first attempt, I have contemplated the correct answer...So this time I told her, 'Mommy, sight is very important to everybody, so it must be our eyes.' She looked at me and told me, 'You are learning fast, but the answer is not correct because there are many people who are blind.'

Stumped again, I continued my quest for knowledge, and over the years, Mother asked me a couple more times, and always her answer was, 'No. But you are getting smarter every year, my child...' Then one year, my grandfather died. Everybody was hurt. Everybody was crying. Even my father cried.

I remember that especially because it was only the second time I saw him cry. My Mom looked at me when it was our turn to say our final goodbye to my Grandfather. She asked me, 'Do you know the most important body part yet, my dear??'

I was shocked when she asked me this now. I always thought this was a game between her and me.

She saw the confusion on my face and told me, 'This question is very important. It shows that you have lived in your life. For every body part you gave me in the past, I have told you were wrong and I have given you an example of why. But today is the day you need to learn this important lesson...'

She looked down at me as only a mother can.

I saw her eyes well up with tears. She said, 'My dear, the most important body part is your shoulder...' I asked, 'Is it because it holds up my head??'

She replied, 'No, it is because it can hold the head of a friend or a loved one when they cry. Everybody needs a shoulder to cry on sometime in life, my dear. I only hope that you have enough love and friends that you will always have a shoulder to cry on when you need it...'

Moral of the Story:

"The most important body part is not a selfish one. It is made for others and not for yourself. It is sympathetic to the pain of others. People will forget what you said. People will forget what you did. But people will never forget how you made them feel."

Chapter - 20

"Mother's Love for a Boy"

"A mother's love is like no other. It's a bond that cannot be broken, a love that cannot be explained, and a feeling that will last a lifetime."

One day Thomas Edison came home and gave a paper to his mother. He told her, "My teacher gave this paper to me and told me to only give it to my mother." His mother's eyes were tearful as she read the letter out loud to her child, "Your son is a genius. This school is too small for him and doesn't have enough good teachers to train him. Please teach him yourself."

Many years after Edison's mother had died, Edison became one of the greatest inventors of the century. One day he was going through the old closet and he found a folded letter that was given to him by his teacher for his mother. He opened it. The message written in the letter was, "Your son is mentally ill. We cannot let him attend our school anymore. He is expelled."

Edison became emotional reading it and then he wrote in his diary, "Thomas Alva Edison was a mentally ill child whose mother turned him into the genius of the century."

Moral of the Story:
"A Mother's love and upbringing can help change the destiny of a child."

Chapter - 21

"*Making Relations Special*"
"Mother's love is peace. It need not be acquired, it need not be deserved."

When I was a kid, my Mom liked to make breakfast food for dinner now and then. And I remember one night in particular when she had made dinner after a long, hard day at work. On that evening so long ago, my Mom placed a plate of eggs, sausage, and extremely burned biscuits in front of my dad. I remember waiting to see if anyone noticed! Yet all Dad did was reach for his biscuit, smile at my Mom, and ask me how my day was at school. I don't remember what I told him that night, but I do remember watching him smear butter and jelly on that biscuit and eat every bite!

When I got up from the table that evening, I remember hearing my Mom apologize to my dad for burning the biscuits.

And I'll never forget what he said: "Honey, I love burned biscuits."

Later that night, I went to kiss Daddy good night and I asked him if he liked his biscuits burned. He wrapped me in his arms and said, "Your Momma put in a hard day at work today and she's real tired. And besides — a little burned biscuit never hurt anyone!"

Moral of the Story:

"Life is full of imperfect things and imperfect people. I'm not the best at hardly anything, and I forget birthdays and anniversaries just like everyone else. But what I've learned over the years is that learning to accept each other's faults - and choosing to celebrate each other's differences - is one of the most important keys to creating a healthy, growing, and lasting relationship."

Chapter - 22

"Rose for Mother"

"A mother's sacrifice is the greatest expression of love, for she puts her children's needs above her own."

A man stopped at a flower shop to order some flowers to be wired to his mother who lived two hundred miles away. As he got out of his car he noticed a young girl sitting on the curb sobbing. He asked her what was wrong and she replied, "I wanted to buy a red rose for my mother. But I only have seventy-five cents, and a rose costs two dollars."

The man smiled and said, "Come on in with me. I'll buy you a rose." He bought the little girl her rose and ordered his own mother's flowers. As they were leaving he offered the girl a ride home. She said, "Yes, please! You can take me to my mother." She directed him to a cemetery, where she placed the rose on a freshly dug grave.

The man returned to the flower shop, cancelled the wire order, picked up a bouquet, and drove the two hundred miles to his mother's house.

Moral of the Story:

"Life is Short. Spend as much time as you can loving and caring people who love you. Enjoy each moment with them before it's too late. There is nothing more important than family."

Chapter - 23

"Love Your Mother"
**"A mother's love is a miracle that brings light
To our darkest days, hope to our deepest fears,
And joy to our Every moment."**

When you came into the world, she held you in her arms. You thanked her by wailing like a banshee.

When you were 1 year old, she fed you and bathed you. You thanked her by crying all night long.

When you were 2 years old, she taught you to walk. You thanked her by running away when she called.

When you were 3 years old, she made all your meals with love. You thanked her by tossing your plate on the floor.

When you were 4 years old, she gave you some crayons. You thanked her by colouring the dining room table.

When you were 5 years old, she dressed you for the holidays. You thanked her by plopping into the nearest pile of mud.

When you were 6 years old, she walked you to school. You thanked her by screaming, "I'M NOT GOING!"

When you were 7 years old, she bought you a baseball. You thanked her by throwing it through the next-door neighbour's window.

When you were 8 years old, she handed you an ice cream. You thanked her by dripping it all over your lap.

When you were 9 years old, she paid for piano lessons. You thanked her for never even bothering to practice.

When you were 10 years old, she drove you all day, from soccer to gymnastics to one birthday party after another. You thanked her by jumping out of the car and never looking back.

When you were 11 years old, she took you and your friends to the movies. You thanked her by asking to sit in a different row.

When you were 12 years old, she warned you not to watch certain TV shows. You thanked her by waiting until she left the house.

Those Teenage Years

When you were 13, she suggested a haircut that was becoming. You thanked her by telling her she had no taste.

When you were 14, she paid for a month away at summer camp. You thanked her by forgetting to write a single letter.

When you were 15, she came home from work, looking for a hug. You thanked her by having your bedroom door locked.

When you were 16, she taught you how to drive her car. You thanked her by taking every chance you could.

When you were 17, she was expecting an important call. You thanked her for being on the phone all night.

When you were 18, she cried at your high school graduation. You thanked her by staying out partying until dawn.

Growing Old and Grey

When you were 19, she paid for your college tuition, drove you to campus, and carried your bags. You thanked her by saying goodbye outside the dorm so you wouldn't be embarrassed in front of your friends.

When you were 20, she asked whether you were seeing anyone. You thanked her by saying, "It's none of your business."

When you were 21, she suggested certain careers for your future. You thanked her by saying, "I don't want to be like you."

When you were 22, she hugged you at your college graduation. You thanked her by asking whether she could pay for a trip to Europe.

When you were 23, she gave you furniture for your first apartment. You thanked her by telling your friends it was ugly.

When you were 24, she met your fiancé and asked about your plans for the future. You thanked her by glaring and growling............, "Muuhh-there, please!"

When you were 25, she helped to pay for your wedding, and she cried and told you how deeply she loved you. You thanked her by moving halfway across the country.

When you were 30, she called with some advice on the baby. You thanked her by telling her, "Things are different now. "When you were 40, she called to remind you of a relative's birthday. You thanked her by saying you were "really busy right now."

When you were 50, she fell ill and needed you to take care of her. You thanked her by reading about the burden parents have on their children.

And then, one day, she quietly died. And everything you never did came crashing down like thunder. "Rock me, baby, rock me all night long." The hand who rocks the cradle ... may rock the world".

Let us take a moment of the time just to pay tribute and show appreciation to the person called MOM though some may not say it openly to their mother. There's no substitute for her. Cherish every single moment. Though at times she may not be the best of friends, and may not agree to our thoughts, she is still your mother!!!

Your mother will be there for you; to listen to your woes, your bragging, your frustrations, etc. Ask yourself "Have you put aside enough time for her, to listen to her "blues" of working in the kitchen, her tiredness???"

Be tactful, and loving, and still show her due respect, though you may have a different view from hers. Once gone, only fond memories of the past and also regrets will be left.

Last Lesson:

"Do Not Take for Granted the Things Closest to Your Heart. Love Her More Than You Love Yourself. Life Is Meaningless Without Her."

Chapter - 24

"8 Lies of A Mother"
**"A mother's arms are more comforting
than anyone else's."**

The story began when I was a child; I was a son of a poor family. We did not even have enough food. Whenever meal times came, my mother would often give me her portion of rice. While she was removing her rice into my bowl, she would say "Eat this rice, son. I'm not hungry."

That was Mother's First Lie.

I was growing up, my persevering mother gave her spare time to go fishing in a river near our house, she hoped that from the fish she caught, she could give me a little bit of nutritious food for my growth. After fishing, she would cook some fresh fish soup, which raised my appetite. While I was eating the soup, Mother would sit beside me and eat the rest of the fish, which was still on the bone of the fish I had eaten. My heart was touched when I saw that. I then used my chopstick and gave the other fish to her. But she immediately refused and said "Eat this fish, son. I don't really like fish."

That was Mother's Second Lie.

Then, when I was in Junior High School, to fund my studies, my mother went to an economic enterprise to bring some used-match boxes that would need to be stuck together. It gave her some money to cover our needs. As the winter came, I woke up from my sleep and looked at my mother who was still awake, supported by a little candlelight, and with perseverance, she continued the work of sticking some used-match boxes. I said, "Mother, go to sleep, it's late, tomorrow morning you still have to go to work." Mother smiled and said "Go to sleep, dear. I'm not tired."

That was Mother's Third Lie.

The final term arrived…. Mother asked for leave from work in order to accompany me. While the sun was starting to shine strongly, my persevering mother waited for me under the heat for several hours. As the bell rang, which indicated that the final exam had finished, Mother immediately welcomed me and poured me a cup of tea that she had brought in a flask. Seeing my mother covered with perspiration, I at once gave her my cup and asked her to drink too. Mother said "Drink, son. I'm not thirsty!"

That was Mother's Fourth Lie.

After the death of my father due to illness, my poor mother had to play her role as a single parent. She had to fund our needs alone. Our family's life was more complicated. No days without suffering. Our family's condition was getting worse, and a kind uncle who lived near our house assisted me now and then. Our neighbours often advised my mother to marry again. But mother was stubborn and didn't take their advice; she said "I don't need love."

That was Mother's Fifth Lie.

After I had finished my studies and got a job, it was time for my old mother to retire. But she didn't want to; she would go to the marketplace every morning, just to sell some vegetables to fulfil her needs. I, who worked in another city, often sent her some money to help her, in fulfilling her needs, but she would not accept the money. At times, she even sent the money back to me. She said, "I have enough money."

That was Mother's Sixth Lie.

After graduating with a Bachelor's Degree, I then continued to do a Master's Degree. It was funded by a company through a scholarship program. I finally worked in the company. With a good salary, I intended to bring my mother to enjoy her life in the Gulf. But my lovely mother didn't want to bother her son. She said to me, "I'm not used to it."

That was Mother's Seventh Lie.

In her old age, my mother got stomach **cancer** and had to be hospitalized. I, who lived miles away, across the ocean, went home to visit my dearest mother. She lay in weakness on her bed after having an operation. Mother, who looked so old, was staring at me in deep thought. She tried to spread her smile on her face…but it was a noticeable effort. It was clear that the disease had weakened the mother's body. She looked so frail and weak. I stared at my mother with tears flowing. My heart was hurt… so hurt, seeing my mother in that condition. But mother with the little strength she had, said "Don't cry, my dear. I'm not in pain."

That was Mother's Eighth and Last Lie. After saying her eighth lie, my Dearest mother closed her eyes forever…

Epilogue

As we reach the conclusion of "The Heart-Touching Stories of Mother's Love," we are reminded that the tales we have explored together are not just stories; they are heartfelt testaments to the incredible bond between mothers and their children. Each narrative has offered a glimpse into the myriad ways that love manifests—through nurturing, teaching, sacrificing, and unwavering support.

In a world that often rushes by, this collection serves as a poignant reminder to pause and appreciate the profound impact of a mother's love. These stories have taken us on a journey through laughter, tears, and shared experiences, reflecting the beauty and complexity of motherhood. They echo the sentiment that while every mother's journey is unique, the essence of love remains universal, transcending boundaries of culture, language, and time.

As you close this book, I encourage you to carry these stories with you. Let them inspire you to celebrate the mothers in your life, whether they are biological, adoptive, or chosen. Take a moment to express your gratitude, share your memories, and recognize the sacrifices made by those who have shaped your life.

The love of a mother is a legacy that lives on in the hearts of her children. It is a love that inspires us to be better, to strive for greatness, and to extend kindness to others. May you find comfort in knowing that the heart of a mother beats within us all, guiding us as we navigate our own paths.

Thank you for joining me on this journey through the heart-warming stories of motherhood. May these tales continue to resonate within you, reminding us all of the incredible power of a mother's love and the enduring connections that bind us together.

With heartfelt appreciation,

OP Sharma

ABOUT THE AUTHOR

Meet OP SHARMA: A Visionary Leader and Catalyst for Change...

OP Sharma is a dynamic and visionary individual who is at the forefront of the Turning Point Foundation. Devoting his life to developing leaders with a mission to make a lasting impact, Sharma is an author, motivational speaker, life skill coach, educationist, trainer, and business development expert. His multifaceted approach has inspired countless individuals on their journey to personal and professional excellence.

Born into a family that valued education and community service, Sharma's early life experiences fuelled his passion for empowering others. Armed with degrees in Management, Law, and Public Administration, he embarked on a mission to combine academic knowledge with a profound understanding of human behaviour and leadership dynamics.

In 2000, Sharma founded the Turning Point Foundation, dedicated to shaping the leaders of tomorrow. Through innovative programs and strategic initiatives, the organization focuses on developing leadership skills that extend beyond boardrooms, emphasizing compassionate and inclusive leadership to create positive societal change.

Sharma's magnetic presence on stage and ability to connect with diverse audiences have made him a sought-after motivational speaker. His talks, infused with real-world anecdotes and practical insights, inspire individuals to overcome challenges, embrace change, and strive for personal and professional growth.

As a life skill coach, Sharma guides individuals on a transformative journey toward self-discovery and personal mastery. His coaching sessions delve into critical life skills, including resilience, effective communication, and emotional intelligence, fostering a holistic approach to personal development.

Sharma's commitment to education is evident in his advocacy for progressive best educational practices. He collaborates with schools, colleges, and universities, championing programs that instil leadership values in students, leaving a lasting impact on the next generation of leaders. Known for dynamic and interactive training sessions, Sharma has honed the skills of individuals across various industries. His customized training programs focus on leadership development, team building, and effective communication, providing practical tools for professionals to excel in their respective fields.

Sharma's keen insights into business development have catalysed growth in Multilevel Marketing. His strategic guidance and innovative approaches have led to successful collaborations, increased profitability, and sustainable business practices.

In the world of leadership development, OP Sharma stands as a beacon, guiding individuals and organizations toward meaningful change. His roles as an author, speaker, coach, educationist, trainer, and business development expert converge to create a tapestry of influence, ensuring that the Turning Point mission continues to shape leaders capable of making a lasting difference in the world.